The

Book of
Poetry

The

Book of Poetry

by

Dave Kapell and Sally Steenland

Workman Publishing
New York

"This Is Just to Say" by William Carlos Williams, from *Collected Poems*:
1909-1939, *Volume I*. Copyright ©1938 by New Directions Publishing
Corp. Reprinted by permission of New Directions Publishing Corp.

Many books were invaluable sources as we developed the writing exer-
cises. *Wishes, Lies, and Dreams* by Kenneth Koch was filled with great
ideas, as were many books from The Teachers & Writers Collaborative.
They include: *Educating the Imagination*, edited by Christopher Edgar
and Ron Padgett; *Handbook of Poetic Forms*, edited by Ron Padgett; and
Poetry Everywhere, by Jack Collom and Sheryl Noethe. Also helpful was
The Practice of Poetry, edited by Robin Behn and Chase Twichell.

Thanks to Adam Van Buren of Northboro Middle School, Northboro,
Massachusetts, for the poem on page 107.

We gratefully acknowledge contributors to this book for permission to
print their poems. Every effort has been made to contact contributors. If
any required credits have been omitted, it is completely unintentional,
and we will gladly correct any omissions in further reprints.

The magnetic poetry book of poetry : an anthology of poems from the
refrigerator doors of America : plus a poetry primer and portable word
pack / by Dave Kapell and Sally Steenland
    p.   cm.
ISBN 0-7611-0737-1
1. American poetry—20th century.
I. Kapell, Dave.
II. Steenland, Sally
PS615.M374   1997   97-22179
811' .5406—dc21   CIP

Workman books are available at special discounts when purchased in
bulk for premiums and sales promotions as well as for fund-raising or
educational use. Special editions can also be created to specification.
For details, contact the Special Sales Director at the address below.

Workman Publishing Company, Inc.
708 Broadway
New York, NY 10003-9555

Printed in Hong Kong
First printing October 1997
10 9 8 7 6 5 4 3 2

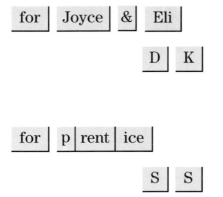

for Joyce & Eli

D K

for p rent ice

S S

contents

The Attraction of Magnetic Poetry

by Robert Pinsky, *Poet Laureate*

When you see these little words scattered on a refrigerator door, and feel a desire to shuffle them around, you are responding to some of the deepest urges in the human animal. That itch to change things as they are into something different and the related itch to play with meaning seem to characterize us as a species. The words, attractively ready to be rearranged, are—magnetic. The word "poet" is based on the Greek word for "maker," which suggests that the artist in us is deeply related to the tinkerer, the gadget-rigger who feels an urge to pile one stone upon another, or to try how a fig leaf might look if we wore one right *here*. Poetry extends that restless making-instinct into the realm of language.

Our tools and our language: these inventions, and the inventiveness behind them, have allowed the species to survive despite its pathetic physical equipment in the way of claws, teeth, hide, and our feeble abilities to run, climb, swim. The little strips of Magnetic Poetry represent in their amiable,

unpretentious invitation both a kind of tool
and a kind of language.

"But you're limited to the words they
give you."

Limitation is one of the things the poet in
us likes. As Rudolf Arnheim says in his
great book *Film as Art*, limitation brings
out the difference between the artist and
the engineer. Confronted with a limitation
(silent film, black-and-white), the engineer
tries to create a way to remove it. Con-
fronted with the same limitation, the artist
tries to create a way to use it (Buster
Keaton, *film noir*).

So, while the engineers at the company that
makes the product have come up with a kit
for making any word you like, with rub-on
letters, artists in their kitchens have amused
themselves and their friends by improvising
with what they have. In my house, we make
magnetic poems and captions to go with
the photographs posted on the fridge door,
and the patching-it-together feeling is part
of the fun: "Languid stare of tiny death god-
dess" and "Man sleeps"—I'm not sure who
wrote them, but there they are—get some
of their feeling from the pressure to invent,
embodied by the slightly cockeyed angles
of the words on their separate strips. I
think that the look of the medium—half
ransom note, half drunken typesetter—may

help encourage us to compose. The words on their magnetic strips help free us to string words together, not only by reducing the intimidating vastness of the whole language, but by their improvised, slapped-together look. The handsomely printed black characters on their bright white background are the straight man, and our goofy compositions, bobbing at a kilter, are the gag-making partner, Gracie Allen to the typographical George Burns.

And both halves of that team, the sober printed characters and the giddy, particular dance of the words, allude to the medium where the poem has its real power: in a human voice, speaking the sounds of the words aloud, whether reading them from the steel appliance door in someone's kitchen, reciting them in an intimate setting, or chanting them at the campfire. The characters always refer to the origin of language, where it is made in the human body, with its breath.

One of the most misapplied terms in contemporary life is "popular art." Many things called by that name are mass-produced, designed and distributed by elite experts, and only some of what they produce becomes popular even in the passive sense of "much purchased." In what sense are each new TV season's failed sitcoms and crime dramas "popular art"? Even the rare

success in the field is not "popular" in the sense that the poems we assemble on our refrigerators are: the compositions of actual American people, produced not for profit but for the fun of it, and to satisfy that peculiar, deep itch to make something new.

R.P.

Preface

The story of Magnetic Poetry begins with a sneeze. In 1993 I was an aspiring songwriter with what would turn out to be three very fortunate problems: chronic writer's block, severe springtime allergies, and seemingly insurmountable student loan debt. One evening I tried to alleviate the first problem by cutting apart newspaper articles and journal entries and rearranging the paper words, a method that can sometimes spark ideas for song lyrics.

That's when the second problem intruded: I sneezed, scattering all of my carefully arranged little slips of paper, obliterating my potential inspiration.

Inspiration of another sort came at that moment, however. I found a stack of fridge magnets advertising a local pizza joint. Why not glue a small piece of magnet to the back of each word? Friends loved my word magnets and stood at the refrigerator door for hours, composing poems and suggesting ways to improve the assortment.

Then the third problem arose—the student loan payment. I needed cash, fast. Maybe I could make a bunch of "poetry kits" and sell them at craft fairs. Could work.

Did work! It worked so well, I found I had a business on my hands. Soon after, I had a wife, a son, and many other wonderful things in my life, including poetry.

And one of the most gratifying parts of all this has been the feedback I get from the people who use Magnetic Poetry and generously share their creations with me. One woman told me, "I'm an 80-year-old great-grandmother, and your product helped me find a part of me I never knew existed. . ." That one alone pretty much made my year, and there have been many more like it.

So thanks, and may the magnetic muse be with you!

D.K.

Wonderful magnetic poetry was out there waiting to be shared. When Dave and I began to spread the word that we were seeking submissions for a book of magnetic poems, the response was tremendous. Over a thousand people sent us their poems, jamming the mailbox and clogging the Internet. The poems came from first-graders and grandmothers, stockbrokers, lawyers, economists, teachers, teenagers, photographers, and ex-hippies.

They were often accompanied by letters telling us how and why the poems were made. Researchers at the Federal Reserve Bank of San Francisco wrote:

"Most of our time is spent programming complex statistical and econometric models that try to shed light on the U.S. and California economy and the banking industry. Magnetic Poetry is the perfect antidote to vector autoregressions, impulse response functions, multinomial probits and adjustments for heteroskedasticity."

"Wow," we said. Incomprehensible jobs— great poems!

One woman submitted poetic messages she composes on the fridge for her family, like this one for her daughter:

> but raise your magic voice to bellow
> like fire into the sun
> I will come home
> mother

With so many to choose among, how did we make our selections? We looked for poems that were vivid, fresh, poignant, funny, lyrical: poems that succeeded in what they set out to do.

Some were one-liners, such as "fast tongues can trip." Others were musings, such as "sun without rain, only part of the

picture." Some aimed for simple rhyme:

> purple must think
> blue always dreamed
> of pink

Many others depended on more complex images and rhythms.

Reading through all the poems so enthusiastically submitted, we realized that Walt Whitman was right. We absolutely could hear America singing—the lusty, varied, exuberant songs of daily life.

S.S.

Warning: Magnetic Poetry can be habit-forming. If reading the work of other magnetic poets inspires you to create your own, please use the magnetic-poetic tools included in this book:

• A poetry primer providing directions and suggestions for different kinds of poems, ways to approach the making of poetry, and tips and techniques especially appropriate to magnetic poetry;

• A portable "starter set" of words, including some not found in any other Magnetic Poetry kit, and a magnet-friendly front cover.

Keep this book close to you—poetry can strike at any time, anywhere. You'll want to be ready whether you're in a café or a Laundromat or in line at the bank. And send us your best poems—we'd like to read them.

Beginnings

Setting out and starting over: Pregnancy, birth, and babies. The expectations and delights of the new.

I was shot from an egg
& soared from mothers bed
like a knife through wax

Ellen Cassedy

In the Moon Palace

wrapped in snow soft as cotton wool
unwrinkled
unconcerned unrepentant
toes warm
wide eyes frosted by haloes of winter
      cloud
belly still
younger than my children
I shall perhaps never
risk an uncoiled rope
never link or permit
unmarked feet to feel the ground

Susan Terris

<u>Butterfly</u>

my not born baby daughter
dances naked in a womans warm belly
she is a wild child
she is a pink embrace inside a wet
      cocoon

John Ottaviano

he tells her he wants a child and a
      babygirl grows
on a little tree like an apple

Student at Ecole de Commerce, Switzerland

<u>Haiku</u>

man	woman
magnificent	spark
baby	boy

Peter Rillero

winter baby
skin like snow
smooth and bare
hair like honey
the color of the summer sky
beneath her feet
are the dreams of the day
gardens of the night
moon child

Alice Shelburne (age 15)

celebrate waking
with dazzled eyes
with childish secret
        joy
boys and old women
are born to it
sacred fools who
voice our universe
as we squirm
in their magic

A. Dupris

she is a fiddle
born chirping
laughing lucky
and warm

a drunk who needs
sweat
songs
and baseball

her random memories whisper
mothers faded milk
and baking bread
blue secrets

behind chocolate lips
scream like fireworks
I am
strong in heart

Lauren Kaushansky

a fat pink cocoon
glowed on that big day
it whispered in the night
that followed

time and sun fed my baby
with moon dreams and
slow cool mud
she was born in a round garden
and flew to a cloud of music
where hot flowers grow
and joy twirls gladly

her song is at once
smart funny and telling

Ted Ringer

our brother & son
the blue eyed angel boy child
with a drooly honey drunk smile
a vision of beauty
like a warm puppy

Peggy Moody
(about her 6-month-old son, Joey)

sweetly
with tiny tripping feet
he blows through the day
like wind
pounding light
beating time
never still

sun boy
playing fast
and falling away
into moon
and bed

Audrey Niffenegger

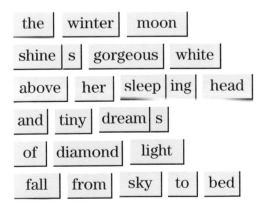

the winter moon
shine s gorgeous white
above her sleep ing head
and tiny dream s
of diamond light
fall from sky to bed

Bruce Levenstein

my daughter
how easy you flew
          blazed
          steamed
          sailed
          away
cut clean the breath
leaving worry
to wake me with salt fever

Phyllis Tashlik

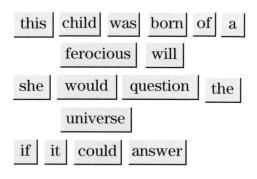

this child was born of a
ferocious will
she would question the
universe
if it could answer

Anonymous

8

Daily Life

Observations on the ordinary: Work, shopping, TV, and food. Thoughts on welding transformed by the refrigerator's white space. Unexpected views of familiar objects.

> ❝ *We are research associates in the Economic Research Department of the Federal Reserve Bank of San Francisco. When we need a break to clear our heads, relax, or just let off steam, we roll our chairs over to the metal filing cabinet on which our poetry resides and compose....* ❞

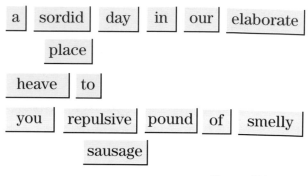

a sordid day in our elaborate place

heave to

you repulsive pound of smelly sausage

Group Effort

Ode to Shoe Shopping

I stare
I worship & drool
do they have my size
frantic I want
I scream when the woman says
no tiny feet

Deanna Brock

Tabloid Tale

puppy panting near a pole
roses raining by the road
woman willing like the wind
suitor screaming to the sun
mother moaning at the moon
honey heading for a hit
goddess going as a gift
love lusting from the lake
finger fluffing in her friend
beauty boiling butter on his bed

Eugene B. Bergmann

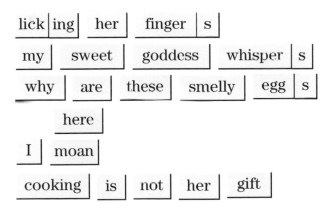

lick ing her finger s
my sweet goddess whisper s
why are these smelly egg s
here
I moan
cooking is not her gift

Stephen Diehl

{ *Magnetic poets talk back lyrically to the TV. They respond to its drone with a pull (or punch) of their own. There are no couch potatoes here . . . .* }

TV

my TV is death
     in a thousand bitter moments
& fluff
      stare and worship its vision
           let it dream for you
     it will use you
& take your
         delicate shadow
           to its bleak garden

Kyle Cassidy

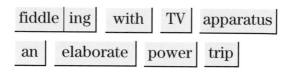

fiddle ing with TV apparatus an elaborate power trip

Donna J. Moore

and the day will ask

how did you use your
arms (two) and legs (same)

if you answer I hit and beat
with rocks and poles
each blow to show how
to truly pound him and his

day will say rip out
your TV

M.K. Streznewski

About Welding

a symphony of blows
the boiling of water
the essential drive
can urge the hot iron
into a beautiful rose petal

Robin MacSwain

spring days sing with delicious light
sunshine boys fly out the screen door
dressed in bare arms and legs
they live a fast beat
their hits and runs going going gone
raw juices storm beneath their skin
and visions of a hot summer
murmur on cool bedtime breezes

how I love these gorgeous moments
for life is sweet music in a windy sky
and peach petals on my tongue

Cynthia J. Lee

sing and worship
egg and sausage
from the cook
and tell her
it is lovely

Bonnie Ferron

Country Club

only the easy can sing
in their blue dresses
cool ones who milk
those next to them for gossip
never asking about above
or below and certainly not
asking the ugly
why
not ever

hairless skin feet the proper size
they sip scotch and water
trip home to honey drunk
running to and from sad lust bare beds

ask Icarus about hot sun
melting wax falling

M. K. Streznewski

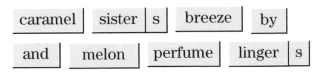

Louise V. Grey

go go girl
did did dress

for cool car club
after eating
rocky road

beat boys
blue music
may mean
any think

do do do
you want to drive me there?

Emily Bristow

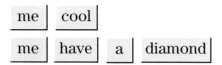

Deanna Brock

how chocolate manipulates
a girls dress size

Donna J. Moore

❝ *Am pleased to enclose a copy of 'essentially repulsive language by means of Magnetic Poetry,' in which my housemates and I have collected our best mag poems for a poetry reading on Lord Byron's birthday.* ❞

two boys sit and watch TV
they say cool
and we want music to rock
they do not think
their heads are void
they always beat
and dream of breasts
still they do not get it
no one wants to be like them
but
                        he he you said
butt

Kyle Cassidy, Brad Hafford, and Jean Pierre Beugoms (with picture of Beavis and Butt-Head)

{ *A remarkable number of magnetic poets brew thoughts into poems as they sip their morning fuel, a potion of coffee and words.* }

potent joe

for the

winter madness

John Brode

I taste
my caffeine morning
with desire and need
pour me
a life pot

Dava Silvia

your ice is at my sacred ground
and the black morning tastes
like a headache
I'd willfully wake for fuel
he brews power
pouring lifc into me
with needy flavor and creamed magic
drinking calm mud I smell strong

Lori A. Koenig

coffee steam morning
I am away but present
picture my hands home

Michael Cohen

Haiku

coffee breath moment
pick animal sacrifice
sausage ghost and egg

Steve Tiffany

A Teacher's Winter Plea

magic winter
where is the cool
dreaming of snow days
imagining home
my cocoon

Elizabeth Hall

never worry
when I go
I will always
let you no
my time home
& wear I go
trust me
you'll see

Charlotte Wilson

66 Can you tell that I am a graduate student? 99

take random naps to recall symptoms
of good life that is long gone
mental pressure is acute
trudge to school open your books
long afternoon work is lousy
has these girls behind in sleep
student hours test laughter work to death
it sucks
sunshine & peace only delicate
memories
I think I am giving up if learning
makes my heart & smile old   and
my eyes shadowed

Laura Tomoko Komai

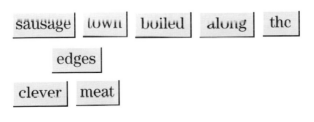

Kelle Schillachi

the mother never dreamed her boys
& girls would milk to sleep and smell
like fluff   or how a cry is like
a knife   and blood the chain of life
yet she will do what woman must
produce   and love not overly
be like a rock   but still not crush
and smooth the going   and then let go

L. McDevitt

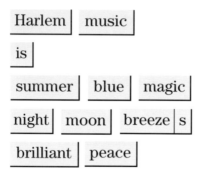

Harlem   music
is
summer   blue   magic
night   moon   breeze s
brilliant   peace

Mahazi Roundtree

give me a can of beer and that last slice
        of chocolate cake
I'm going back to rome

Kami Chisholm

those who clean naked

never laugh at porcelain

but live to lather

Steve Tiffany

stop cook

my finger was raw meat
under a knife

luscious and sweet as honey
moaning

red as rust
sweating

white as wax
boiling

juicy
and delicate as death

Emily Bristow

her watch was so delicate
that the perfume
of the roses
in the warm garden breeze
could stop its hands
time would go still
and freeze

Audrey Niffenegger

did you see
three green bugs
eating coffeecake flowers
& squirming on bellies
as they danced to the beat
of caramel kisses
from here to their hole

Elizabeth Oakley

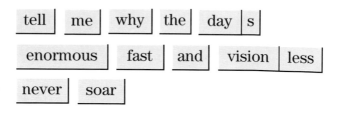

tell me why the day s
enormous fast and vision less
never soar

Suda Skyrus

Love

Love, lust, longing, and lingering resentment—the most popular themes of many magnetic poets. The public nature of the refrigerator door seems to invite intimate declarations.

if she asks about the rose
lie
say the languid ache behind your breast
     is a petal still pink and sleeping
     in a bed for two

Judi K. Beach

YES: An Acrostic Haiku

you	drive	me	so	mad
every	time	you	lie	then
say	please	forgive	me	

Charles West

Love Poem #4

these are the dreams we left
on loves blue pillow
under the film of time

they are lighter than the tree branch
the wind shakes this morning

I can smell their shadowing
I can feel your neck a silken
ache around which beauty climbs and
        glitters

one is the dream in which you stand
        before me
breathing so lusciously
the stars weep around your head
like yellow goddess eyes

in the other whole forests
imitate my body
rocking gently upright in pure madness

even the wind there crying love
turns its thousand powers into music

Gail Wronsky

you move like some
grass bug woman
     god naked from sex
sacrificing your heat
     for one moist kiss
closed in my warm rhythm
     stiff
          wet
               belly magic
    a hard
          broken animal
squirming with
     hot bone fever
for you

Mounya

I like bare easy lusty men
whispering in my bed
only these think of love play
in symphony and shadow
beneath the hot blood
of the winter moon

Nicki Serquinia

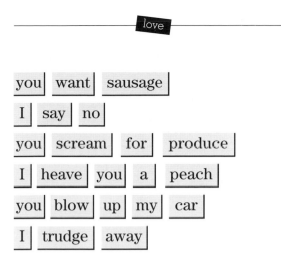

you want sausage
I say no
you scream for produce
I heave you a peach
you blow up my car
I trudge away

Stephen Diehl

like a thousand tongues chanting
I I I I I
read the honey juice light
in your hair

it felt cool
it was like
smooth and sweet

music
like
over the top
and like
going going gone

Emily Bristow

boy
after I pool you out
in to
streams
which run like grass
you
still
haunt me
as poison
devours my mornings
boy
listen
to me melting
and let me
hold you

Sara Femenella (age 16)

Laurence McGilvery

drive with me in to spring
>road trip   red hot   raw visions
>languid water light like a gift
>lazy essential urges
>easy love beneath a waxing
>>moon
>purple shadow music   sit under
>>bare sky   whisper
>less drool please

Christine Paige

hot pants
fiddle gown
purple pound
latherly luscious
shake it girl
not so fast
go on gorgeous
tell me how you like it
want on
never stop

Megan Hester

men are bitterness
but I say
my ugly delirious man
is wantless chocolate

he robs me
of my tiny petals
and who I am

together we whisper
of when I felt the sea
in the blue moon

like a diamond
in a forest of moments

with my bare feet
and his shadow
of cool mists

do take the powerful road
or go mad

Hannah Lewis (age 16)

❝ *It's a love poem for my husband Tony, and for all of those who have been married a long time but still remember and occasionally recapture those early, heady days of falling in love . . . .* **❞**

do you recall those summer days
drunk like honey
delirious lazy languid

life goes on
we need milk eggs juice time
please
but we sleep dream love yet
still mad about you

Sara Latta

cook up some
sun d a es
& lust

Christine Paige

you watch TV most
on days when he
is worshiping
a woman
who is
not you

a ripped rose dress
and cool smooth skin

put his dream breast to rest
with a click

Adrienne GreenHeart

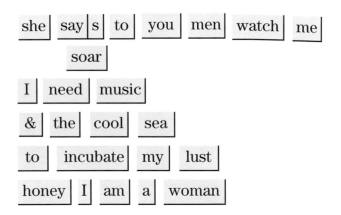

she say s to you men watch me
soar
I need music
& the cool sea
to incubate my lust
honey I am a woman

Rebecca M. Holmes

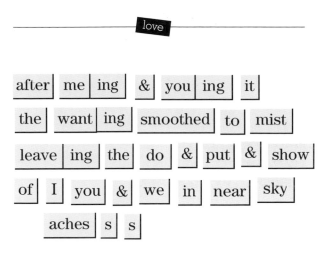

Susan Kan

the bitter winter storm
will always produce a delirious spring
symphony
so think about a fall with me
in love next summer

Bennett J. Berson

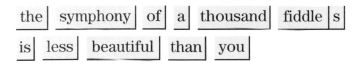

Amy Lythgoe

I see
     an elaborate woman
  she sits in a cool blue place
and all she has
  goes for an arm and a leg
they want two thousand
  for a raw egg
     incubated in her hair
I think
she has
diamonds
    in her head
it is said
    true beauty is in her blood
    and power is in her scream

Brad Hafford

never one to sweat
my friend is in a lather
panting and heaving
trudging after love

Jennifer Soller

a thousand roses will not do

I ache for the smell of you

Susan Johnson

we lie in the moist green grass and
    whisper of perfume and poetry
    soon time melts you and I are the
    universe

Sarah McNay (age 18)

I tell cows

about you

Iver Fischman

if you were a
flower
I'd eat you
freely
slowly
lingering
on your
velvety soft
lips
celebrating
as
my breath danced
in & out
like the rhythm
of a wild
ocean breeze

Charlotte Wilson

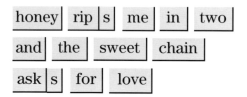

Hannah Lewis (age 16)

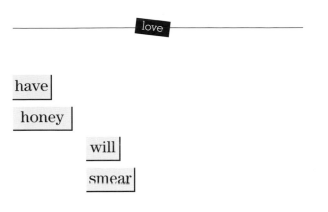

have

honey

will

smear

Sora Counts

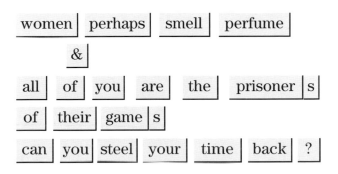

women perhaps smell perfume
&
all of you are the prisoner s
of their game s
can you steel your time back ?

Dimitriy Vasilevskiy (age 13)

she walks beside me
like jazz
coming over the backyard
fence on a warm
sunday morning

David Mark Greaves

please whisper
puppy boy
my hair aches
and I am sleepless

Rita Volpi

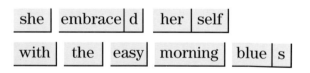

she | embrace | d | her | self
with | the | easy | morning | blue | s

Justina Willis

o mother
I am not the girl
you would have me be
I am a woman delirious in love
frantic in language sweetly
crushed together
with whisper and shadow
I sing and dream and love
as though shot through with light
and diamonds shining bitterly
watch me mother
I smear your breast
with the honey milk of my sun

Dawn Ennis Crocetti

speak of this place and soar above
like a thousand angels
you were worshiped in love

Pam McNay

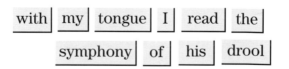

her leg is made of water, of roses and
lies and a gown of shadows
and you want to take it in your teeth
and howl into the night

Teresa Breeden

I am woman
& must not trudge
after him

Ellen Cassedy

with my tongue I read the
symphony of his drool

Deanna Brock

to please her
        I am incubating a head
in the garden
        it will produce elaborate rock
                music
        like she worships
                & boil a man to death
                in chocolate

Kyle Cassidy

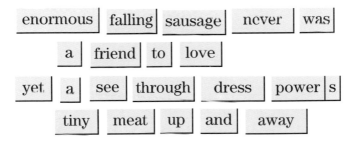

Stephen Diehl

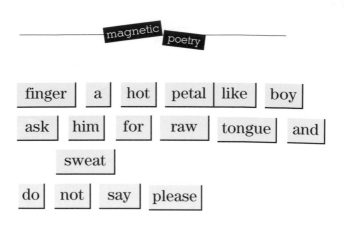

Suda Skyrus

their wild night behind them
they boil chocolate
and remember the wind and rain

Steve Tiffany

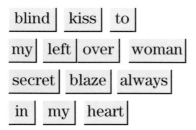

Kevin Scott Engstrom

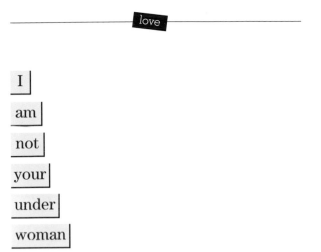

I
am
not
your
under
woman

Rita Volpi

you wear desire
like a poison
deep within your heart

Jamie Darsey

I need a he

Kasey Abler

we lie abreast avoiding asking
staring away together
you think of hot mad ugly
bitterness you could say
want to say
but have not yet said
and after all here in my bed
under weak moonlight
the need is stilled
a spring wind blows through
a cool whisper of death
we draw closer

Audrey Niffenegger

my sweet elaborate boy
I dreamed you in
a thousand summer shadows
always luscious
never easy
I loved you in spring rains
together felt like worship
we must take time
to recall it all

Candace B. Gallagher

Nature

The cycle of seasons, bugs and
butterflies, gardens and stars.
The rhythms of the natural world
inspire the rhythm of words.

Sea Language

cool trudging
      one two
a chant of fluff and lather

blue rips to white
the spray whispers swim

urges
like a tongue
licking your bare life
to a scream

Lisa Roullard

I am berry crazy
bursting kisses of blue pearls
pervading wishes born at summers
axis rippling into fall

A. Dupris

66 *We are Galen (age 9) and his mom Cathie Gilbreath. We have had great fun and even teary moments enjoying the things that we have written . . . .* **99**

winter flew down silent
green spring nests big
it is not born yet
the twirly snow ate the sky
it flew down
fat and silent
funny cool magic around my home
nesting
whispering white
joy came in depths

Cathie Gilbreath

the yellow star and yellow sun
big glow ing
dark blue color dream ing
for one magic spring

Galen Gilbreath

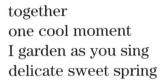

together
one cool moment
I garden as you sing
delicate sweet spring

Kristy Hylbert (age 12)

the winter night is cool
and the sky is cloudy
the snow is whispering by the trees

Jenna Mitby
(Thoreau Elementary School,
Madison, Wisconsin)

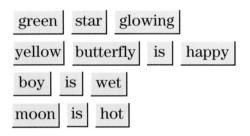

green star glowing
yellow butterfly is happy
boy is wet
moon is hot

Matt Cyrus
(Thoreau Elementary School,
Madison, Wisconsin)

66 *When I asked my son Danny about this poem, he said, 'For kids, sometimes clouds in a storm look bitter, like coffee. And the rain makes things rust and grow.' His next poem was about a 10-legged ant. Go figure.* 99

A Storm

cool and windy
like the white moon above
with the whisper of rain
the sky says not a word
but the wind runs bitter as it whispers
rust and life
as it sings

Danny Krawiec (age 6)

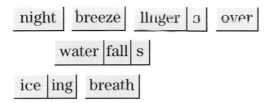

Sarah Blonstein (age 15)

One Peachy Day

smear the white juice
of crushed sunlight
over my breasts
the delirious milk
of summershine
go on tell the sky to
lick me to death
with his hot tongue
of blue music
show him how
to pound out the beat
in my mad blood

all I want is
to sweat topless
under the true language
of skin
legs waxed and lathered
cooking like pink honey

what a trip it is
from here to there

Dianne Borsenik

the goddess
of winter light
fingered the cool water
strummed the waves
into ermine foam

bored she wove
the icy spray
into purple shadow
and spun herself
into a pillar of salty moon

Donna Wahlert

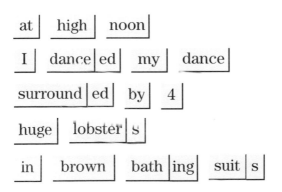

at | high | noon
I | dance | ed | my | dance
surround | ed | by | 4
huge | lobster | s
in | brown | bath | ing | suit | s

Deborah Menit

❝*The poetry corner at my office became a stress-reduction center and a place to get the creative juices going during the work day....***❞**

the rain dreams
of the sea

Marileta Robinson

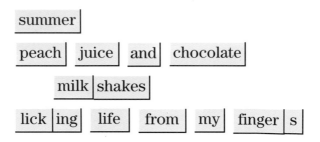

summer

peach juice and chocolate

milk shakes

lick ing life from my finger s

Allison Lassieur

ship these dresses away
the spring wind is my gown

Marileta Robinson

Insighting

there must be
blue light twirling
inside a cocoon

far down slowly
frost and far wings
a winter butterfly

Rod Jellema

Ocean Lives

prisoner fish of the haunted hot deep
      ocean
embraced in a perfume-like smell
two explore warm liquid
in time all
will decay

Adam Birch
(Eighth grade, Kewaskum Middle School,
Wisconsin; Mary Reilly-Kliss, teacher)

you sit
&
lick spring
from under
winters trudge
of shadow

you moan
luscious

Robert K. Giesen

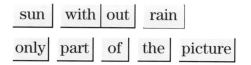

Donna J. Moore

Ages of Man

he loved the winter mother whitely
the girls of spring he dreamed of pinkly
he lusted for the summer woman redly
but falls cool goddess he worshiped
      blackly

Eugene B. Bergmann

only after summer
did I shake it
my feet ached beneath me
when all I did was sit
red from the sunshine
avoiding the next sweet time
it takes a full winter
to want the light

Suda Skyrus

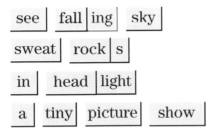

see | fall | ing | sky

sweat | rock | s

in | head | light

a | tiny | picture | show

Melissa Pollack

you blow, day, delirious, like two forests
    inside a petal

Teresa Breeden

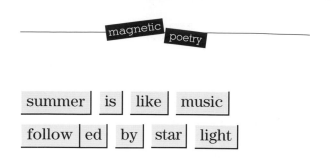

summer is like music
follow ed by star light

Ms. Fink's Class (Homer, Alaska)

spring takes us to water
summer trips us with her lazy beauty
her enormous pink easy finger
showing the way to winters white
    tongue

Jean Aberlin

be still the rain
for it is on the mist
the sun will light at day
taking you to your love
like a water symphony whispering spring
through lifes diamond moment
    recalling a sea shadow
dreaming her sweet stare into falls lusty
    summer storm

Howard O. Lamb, Jr.

I see a rose in a garden
its petals are tiny and red
a light rain falls
down from the sky
and cools its lovely head

Annamarie Zmolek (age 14)

the moon shines like a gift
a smooth white lake of sleep in the
    winter sky
eternity above it
a moments shadow beneath

Bruce Kinzey and Julie Savell

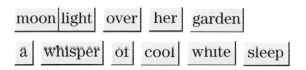

The Hull Family

behind a blue summer sky
when winter smells like spring
you whisper like a butterfly
where is the wind

Stephanie Baumgart (age 13)

the warm summer
sunshine whispers
rhythms in my head
like a chained
prisoner dreaming
of the cool blue
sky

Brian Lunde

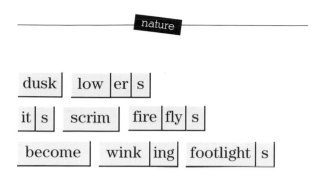

dusk | low | er | s

it | s | scrim | fire | fly | s

become | wink | ing | footlight | s

Donna Wahlert

today
let me please
bare my feet
dress for sunshine
worship spring moon
sky so gorgeous
summer rose garden
blue sea enormous
all gifts from above

Gisella Sizemore

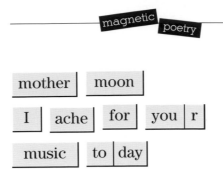

mother moon

I ache for you r

music to day

Laurence McGilvery

who? cried owl
man, whispered turtle
where?
on the lake
fly!
go fast, far!
so he silently flew up to the moon,
winging in the dark sky
flew by cool wet clouds
nested in his tree home
good night

Christie Cahoon (age 8)

Maxims

Whether from Mom or "Anon," these poems speak volumes. Here are tips, aphorisms, attention-getting commands. As with most advice, take them with a grain of salt.

eat a moment like a sausage
use a stare like a knife
crush time by worshiping light
drool lust like petal juices
recall sweet whispers
ask death over for chocolates
produce spring
manipulate language into symphonys
let love love

Bekka Eaton

leave power to those
who pant after it
we will eat chocolate
bitter for me
sweet for you
easy to say
mad not to do

Suda Skyrus

Song

he |ing| she |ing|

you |ing| me |ing|

laugh |ing| see |ing|

his |ing| her |ing|

am |ing| my |ing|

live |ing| die |ing|

and| all| you| do|

is| sit| ?|

M.K. Streznewski

perhaps our god felt naked
this dance is bitter
laugh fool

Karin Miller

> ❝ We are the McNay family—Sarah (18),
> Pam (Mom), Terry (Dad), Gina (13), and
> Reed (8)—we have lots to send you . . . . ❞

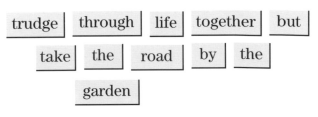

trudge through life together but
take the road by the
garden

Pam McNay

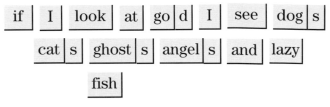

if I look at go d I see dog s
cat s ghost s angel s and lazy
fish

Reed McNay

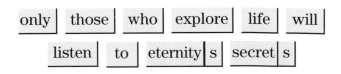

only those who explore life will
listen to eternity s secret s

Pam McNay

power is like a weak mother
it always manipulates an easy moment

Nancy W. Diessner

Boys

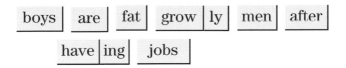

Lisa Ruth Carpinone (age 8)

some worship power
but always want mother
beneath

Charles Sidney Bernstein

{ *Magnetic poets work with words so con-*
cretely, it's no surprise that so many find
their favorite subject to be language itself. }

at poetrys center
a laughing fever
the longing for a language
like liquid rhythm

Melissa Pollack

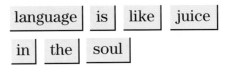

language is like juice
in the soul

Kaya Adams

language is a luscious garden
manipulate the produce

Robert Ingenito

Emily Dickinson

the language goddess
composes
a symphony
of sound

incubates
a moment
sprays
a vision

it disseminates
on the brain

as smooth petals
of truth
ooze
gorgeous
pain

Lisa Hendricks

remembering is the secret of poetry

Rebecca Gabrielle Porath Katz (Age 9)

poetry is
smoky corduroys
purple velvet perfume
sweet rhythm candy
it is
rose rain
and
a shot of iced coffee
with moon light

Juliet Bishop

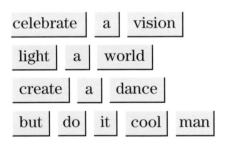

celebrate a vision
light a world
create a dance
but do it cool man

Monika Haupt

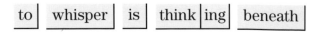

to whisper is think ing beneath

Jeremy Burger

Sacrifice and Broken Fevers

remember when candy was a god thing
how you listened to its voice
desired to know its magic
celebrated caramel secrets
explored every sacred thing
could there have beat
a more trusting heart
but then the dark angel of change
worked his lie
ghosted from hand to eye
killed that wild bone of dazzle

if you put yourself in the smoke
make peace with the lingering fires
blaze harder
than those hot mornings
you will learn to heal
ask poetry
it says come
you can drink my melted smiles
eat of me and be free

Dianne Borsenik

{ *Women can always find space on the refrigerator door to post warnings and words of wisdom—about men . . . .* }

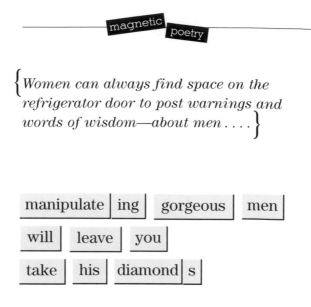

manipulate | ing | gorgeous | men
will | leave | you
take | his | diamond | s

Christine Paige

say boy take time to whisper your love
for your dream woman is one
honey in a thousand

Merle McMorrow

bitterness runs with the shadows of lust

Kelly Running (age 14)

manipulate the moment
always take life as you see it
some will trudge weakly through the void
      not me

Brad Hafford

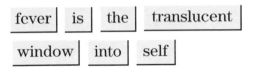

Peter Couch

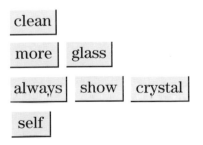

Martin Cole

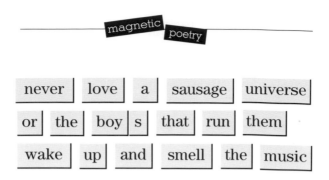

never love a sausage universe
or the boy s that run them
wake up and smell the music

Jamey Jones

celebrate life
find time to give one self a toast

Sherry Lynne Polcyn

listen for the song
that lives in your soul

Elizabeth DiGregorio

delicate girl
        be still
never ask what chains
the sweet goddess must put on

Ann Eastabrooks

darkness | is | light | inside | out

Marylou Imbornone

you will make of the soul which need
        not exist
a woman better than he is

Kami Chisholm

be | hold | I | design | me

Robert K. Ruby II

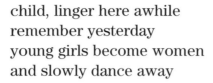

child, linger here awhile
remember yesterday
young girls become women
and slowly dance away

Patricia Willever

soar above the sea
trudge through luscious forests
dream under the sun
smell delicate petals
sing sweet music
read and recall
whisper behind fingers
watch white fluffy skies
shine like diamonds
I'll tell you what its like to live

Katherine Ward (age 13)

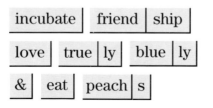

Christine Paige

our feet ran out only

when love did

Jean Aberlin

think sun
say what you want
lather up
drive fast
swim drunk
trudge through your garden
trip
smell crushed roses
moon him
rip one
whisper of raw beauty
want chocolate
play overseas
worship your goddess
watch my butt
live gorgeous moments
be weakless

Peggy O'Neil

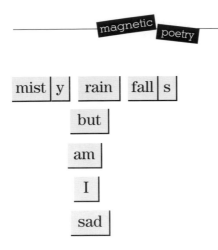

mist | y | rain | fall | s

but

am

I

sad

Brad Hafford

to kiss life softly
free a child
listen & ask a prisoner
breathe every morning
explore
dance
live
love
devour
as always I will
& so you

Christina Girgis

Companions

Those kindred spirits, whether family or
friend, human or animal, who drive us
crazy and keep us warm. Odes and rants
inspired by our nearest and dearest.

she likes having smart funny friends
and a peaceful loving heart
she lives like the sky
luscious enormous and whispering
goddess girl of her magic
upon a diamond cloud
born inside a little white bubble
she likes her rain water castle
and dark jumping shadow
life is good as is

Alice Shelburne (age 15)

The Journey

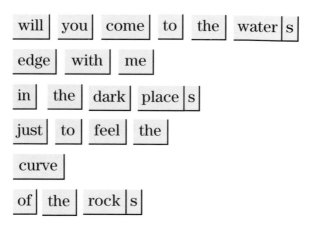

will you come to the water s

edge with me

in the dark place s

just to feel the

curve

of the rock s

Kathleen A. Sawyer

Haiku

do you think I am
repulsive whispering my
love dreams to the cat

Charles West

Celebrating You

our joy knows worry
as you open a present
surrounded in green
we picture a deep down
bitter secret
as we eat
cake

Candace B. Gallagher

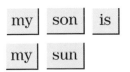

Evelyn Tasch Laurie

frantic puppy moans when she leaves
only wanting a friend to play with
please love me he panted sadly

Lani M. Gallimore

I love you dad and mom
imagine a yellow balloon
in the blue night sky
here comes moon say goodbye
kiss me good night or I'll die

Dorsey Claybourne (age 7)

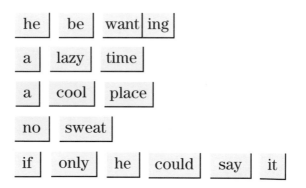

he be want ing
a lazy time
a cool place
no sweat
if only he could say it

Ellen Cassedy

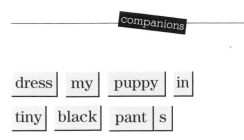
dress my puppy in

tiny black pant s

Lawrence McGilvery

Ocean's Son

born of the deep
you are the oceans son
where a boy once laughed
the old man speaks
with a salty voice
and his smile colors the beach
as worry sails away
upon the current

Robert "Skip" Mills

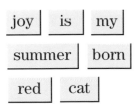

joy is my

summer born

red cat

Lisa Daniels (age 5)

I tell the water
wintering by cool
colored moons

follow me

I soar through smooth blue gardens
like girls frantic
the delicate moans of the sea
boiling easy at my feet

I am weak with lies

sit with me tiny
above mean red skies
ask why and where

we must go
home
so a symphony of those
that love will be born

Linda and Scott Denstaedt
(mother and 12-year-old son)

my brother lingers
in a breeze of
broken smoke
almost free of time
but a prisoner of
moments
bone weak &
flooded with mad life
listening in the dark
for morning

Candace B. Gallagher

Carol Ann Linder

Prayer for My Blind Brother

mother of the concrete ocean
breathe into my blind brother
two translucent window fish

he will eat grass shadows
drink broken glass
devour enormous poles alive

let him throb that fevered stare
all green young men have
for a brilliant blue corduroy woman
     in red

embrace her with squirming TV
     diamonds
give him her wet tongues
dazzling purple steam to kiss

H. Edgar Hix

her lips never will worry
how soft it is
she has feet the color of coffee
and blue blue eyes
she bathes almost never
and questions god

Allen Gerald Helgeson

please
no crying
he will read to you
tiny one

of spring rains
of summer & roses
and winter storms

he will whisper to you
of pink & purple & peach
of dreaming & life
of love and mother
and delicate you

Leslie Hamilton Kapell

Real Men

dressed in friendly blue gowns
      we cooked
      our pant legs
with a rusty apparatus
and crushed the TV
chanting are we not men
after
      I recall ironing fluffy red suits
      to the beat of a delirious symphony

Brad Hafford

silent sister
heart glows and grows
friend and friend
heart and heart
we are together for always
hand in hand

Galen Gilbreath (age 9)

Interiors

The life of the mind—dreams and
musings, fantasy and wit. Whether
dark or light, they're the overheard
conversations inside our heads.

always after the dream
about hair
she cries

it is there
one moment
and in her sleep
she runs the knife
over her bare head
parting only skin

Audrey Niffenegger

I am my mothers sacrifice
and my fathers bitter ache
a daughter born of blood ripe with
        secrets
skin red and blue
breath poisoned with fire
bones broken and haunted
watch me heal

Gina M. Libner

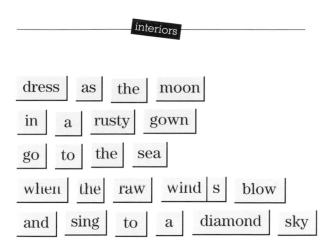

dress as the moon
in a rusty gown
go to the sea
when the raw wind s blow
and sing to a diamond sky

Ellen Cassedy

a
long ago
ghost
of
green
the slow color
that tasted
like eternity
when I was
once
my fathers
little son

Stephen Lindsey

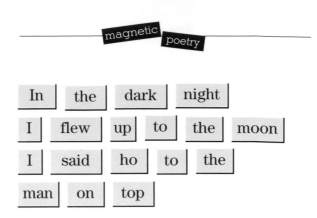

In the dark night
I flew up to the moon
I said ho to the
man on top

Michael
(from Pam Allen's class at North Beach
Elementary School in Seattle, Washington)

dreams
light
sleep

like

sun
licks
water

into
rain

Emily Bristow

{ *Suzanne Berland brought home a display easel along with her MagPo kit. The easel, with its shifting sentences that stretched into stories, wandered from the dining table to her daughter Lara's bedroom, where this poem was completed....* }

a gorgeous woman sits in an
elaborate garden   her beauty is as
sweet and true as a rose petal soaring
in the wind to the sky   she sings a
smooth symphony and whispers
powerful pictures of life into the lake
and lets them swim away   soon she
will have no more dreams or gifts left
to give to anyone   the breeze is cool
as it blows through her hair   the flowers
are covered with fresh dew and the air is
filled with mist   a small dog lies on her
red velvet dress

Lara Berland (age 12)

Brilliant Star

hand to its glass
a blind child questions
the windows blaze
      she listens
as the bushes dance
to the rhythm of a breeze
never to be lifes prisoner,
nor ask who or why
her two dazzling blue eyes
celebrate every brilliant star

Robert "Skip" Mills

purple	must	think
blue	always	dream	ed
of	pink

Candace B. Gallagher

Too Hot to Sleep

on hot summer nights I dream of
wet winter snow
and jumping into bubbly spring
rain water
of fat green frogs playing down
at a cool dark muddy lake
and I imagine happy times
in my garden

Heath Cooper

I am watching
a thousand goddesses
in the mist
of the forest
they have skin like milk
hair like rain
blood like honey
I wish not to be dreaming
then I could sing with them
their sweet summer symphony

Jennifer Nieves

"One morning I came downstairs and found the following poem from my daughter on the refrigerator. Should I worry?**"**

I scream
luscious lazy wax diamonds
blue and red
swimming in drool
I dream
of a forest of enormous sausages
and drunken women
spraying milk
at boys

Justine D'Ooge (age 8)

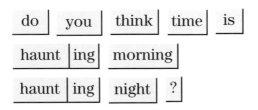

do you think time is
haunt ing morning
haunt ing night ?

Kirk Callison

playing in a castle
one summer night
magic wings grow

like a yellow butterfly
you fly silently
across the sky

I follow slowly
in the clouds
whispering

dream on

David Deutsch (age 7)
and Judith Burstyn (his mom)

a pole shakes its fist at raw love
floods this place with iron
you will build a house of tiny splinters
    from this pole
build a house that shrugs away raw love

Teresa Breeden

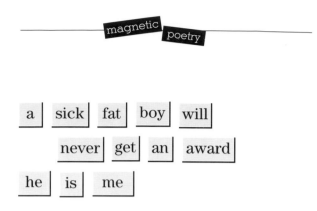

a sick fat boy will

never get an award

he is me

Alexander (age 12)

dreams ache like petals pounding on my
skin

Megan Hester

surrender leaves the floor bowing slightly
        with a delicate laze
ask the moon to dance this time
she is leaning against the wall

Teresa Breeden

Endings

Life's losses, both great and small,
captured in words of regret, loneliness,
and grief that (for a while, at least)
fill the empty spaces.

a fever pierces the angels
they sweat and fly
the next heart is born
I explore the delicate flower of dying

Karin Miller

I ache
said she
the void is like death
the sky is black
and to think I loved you

Jennifer Soller

through a thousand dream s I drive
think ing away a tiny life

Bruce Kinzey and Julie Savell

*66 The kit helped me express my feelings
about a painful loss, that of my beloved
dog Duke, a 10-year-old, sweeter-than-
imaginable Doberman pinscher....99*

light must shine above the bitter void
        my puppy and friend
our life together over and bare
a mother crushed by death
        my boy is gone
                no
        drooling
        rocking
        playing
        licking
        panting
        chocolate
        smelly tongue
                or
        sweetness
his delicate love worshiped me
        he will run like the wind
        I cry here and ache and go away
        sad
        I will always love him

*Ann Nelson
(for Sir Duke of Windsor IV, "Duke,"
June 25, 1986–June 2, 1996)*

Elegy for Delia:
<u>1974 Datsun B-210</u>

she, the car
gone away from this place
and how the man loved her
crying as he sits
blue like she is
let it go
drive always and never stop
you and me and he together
you are true beauty
our friend

Shawna Taylor

<u>Fear</u>

his lip was most still
like a breath
after a dark blind
picture

Connie Cohen

66 *The poem is about my brother—he died in a car accident. I miss him every day. So far I haven't been able to write another poem, but I am optimistic that if I stand by the fridge patiently and with an open mind and heart, the poems will come.* 99

life crushed like leaves
he loved the delicate symphony of
        singing together
the light of a thousand delirious
        diamonds stormed
when he whispered crying above the
        smooth summer road
I ask if some enormous gift is gone
screams no mother tongue yes
here lick the cool sweet milk of
        essential whiteness
rainy blue winter tells him about
        sleeping always
red sky moans and skin aches spring
        shines you said in heaven
no tiny moon deaths please in the garden
        beneath as peach petals play
worshiping dreams the shadow recalls
time could fall panting as
it watches a lovely boy run after a sad
        man and soar

Kate Throop

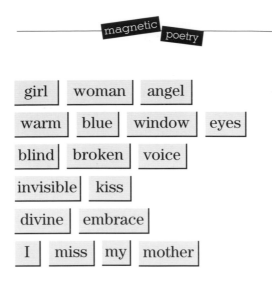

girl woman angel

warm blue window eyes

blind broken voice

invisible kiss

divine embrace

I miss my mother

Amy Greenhill

from the shadows of my dream
                 he springs
he whispers to me
               a symphony
I lick his sweat like
the juice of a luscious peach
the power of death is void
               in sleep
we lie together

Gayle Lin

*66 The day my friend died, I found myself
standing in front of the refrigerator for
two hours piecing together this poem. 99*

Ron

I chant a symphony
about our loving moments
you were still heaving
weak and delirious
moaning in sweat shadowed sleep
through a winters death
a gorgeous sweet man
gone like mist

run without chains
play rock music in the garden
eat only the most luscious there
         but
could you please
recall my picture
whisper when you ask for me
         lie next to me
         place an arm
of enormous blue black sky
wind sun and a delicate rain
my gift from you
a dreaming true love friend

Marykay Czerwiec, RN, ACRN

I picture my shadow falling
      through a pink lake
rose petals swimming
she is crying
      light wind blowing
      spring barely showing
day whispers by
      and for the moment
           no thing aches

Alex Fogelson

Unique Expressions

Jazzy rhymers and zingy one-liners.
Concrete or jigsaw, smorgasbord or
surreal—even when words can't describe
it, magnetic poets are creating it.

winter is as ugly

as an arm hair

Jeremy Hartman

a   is   I
deep   the   do
woody   animal   know
perfume   present   that
surrounds   in   at
her   the   heart
            girl   she'd
                        growl
                        and
                        kill

David C. Gage

miss porcelains father can drink
    champagne like a giant cow

Chris McCormick,
Leawood Middle School

"Fiddle me fingers!" the frantic man
    said.
"The forest is flooding and so is my
    head.
It drives me to sing of love
to tell of two ships at sea
one white as winter sky above
the next as black as me."

Bert & Judith Ellis

Seen—Scene

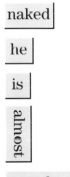

naked

he

is

almost

translucent

C.S. Mahon

{*This poem, the writer tells us in his letter,*
is to be sung to the tune of "The Yellow
Rose of Texas."}

delirious as sex is
its concrete in your cup
the pool of sweat and honey
is ferocious to drink up
for after hair and fingers
and skin and liquid lust
the champagne of pink embrace
        becomes
your present glass of rust

Steve Tiffany

but | he | so

fiddle | butt

and | garden | head

Megan Hester

laugh like lazy licking liquid lips
flooding fat frantic feverish friendly
      forests
with the milk of your tongue

Jamey Jones

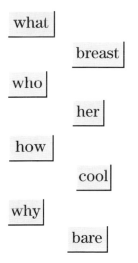

Laurence McGilvery

{ *One of the best parts of making Magnetic Poetry kits in foreign language editions is experiencing the different rhythms and flavors of these French and Spanish poems.* }

Je suis fleur un peu triste et timide
pourtant, rose angélique, insolite
qui se révéle comme un soupir docile . . .
J'ai un royaume, immobile de desir . . .
oublié!
mais une vie inutile
dans le désert toujours vide
torride de soleil . . .
c'est un rêve pale
monotone
glauque
une épine
un chant faible . . .

Yvonne Rall

Dulce Luna

una estrella encendida

hermosos recuerdos

música de fuego
sueños de pasión

como nunca antes

sangre sexual
desnudo calor
que felicidad contigo

un regalo ardiente
en la noche caliente

Vonelle Silvas

{*Magnetic walls installed in six cities
during National Poetry Month gave
passersby a chance to compose amid
the company of strangers . . . .*}

I feel gas coming
rumbling deep inside of me
must be the meatloaf

Robert Zak
*(I composed this impromptu haiku in the
midst of an after-lunch constitutional, the
purpose of which was to settle my stomach.)*

I put down these lines
two or three
hoping someone will
notice me
I stopped a while to sip some tea
sure enough someone
was watching me

William James Tremper (age 69)
*(It was really coffee that I was drinking.
What the hell, I made it rhyme.)*

the breeze presented smoke and fire
      and water
to devour my job in the golden square
my home is in deep flood water in
      Grand Forks
an ocean is devouring my peace
the vast stream has spoiled it
and a cold liquid ghost has made
      beaches of decay
surreal fires bellowed and burned
from the center of my rotting wet
      universe
perhaps god will wake and bring
more green and less blue

Jake Laux, Rich Thelen, Kim Kelly, Ken Kelly
(From the Minneapolis Poetry Wall)

I worry that watching a flower
will bleed away all of my power
to work through my blush
its petals I crush
and open my lips to devour

Steve Tiffany

Melting Concrete

His heart beneath the skin and bone
Is porcelain ice and beats too slow.
If pierced it would not bleed but she
Can warm the knife with whispering.
Can melt his blood with velvet words
That boil his lust with poison urge.
An angel speaking poetry
A drink of liquid symphony
A dance in evening gardens sweet
With haunting looks and naked feet
Milky moonlight falling wet
On flowers moist with summer sweat.
Marble gods stand stiff and wear
A blushing smile and glassy stare.
Above, the stars blaze silently
Devouring every word she breathes
Lingering long in language deep
In fevered moans and perfumed sleep
And so her fire can lick his blood
And change the concrete into flood.

Pam Collins

{*Poet Gail Wronsky asked her writing class to create one-line phrases about famous people using magnetic poetry tiles . . . .*}

Celebrity One-Liners

ELVIS: and they can wax me honey

ELIZABETH TAYLOR: all those mad togetherings behind her

ROSEANNE: you worship sausageness girl

MARILYN: still gorgeous dream goddess

HILLARY: he and I do elaborate power shadow show

JAMES DEAN: if I moan under my bed going drunk and smelling bitter you would say cool

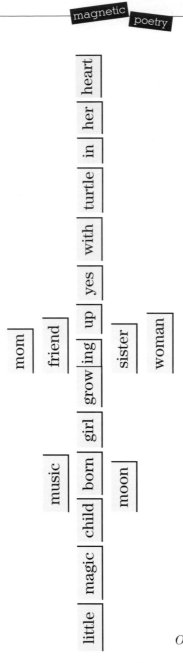

Olive Hagemeier

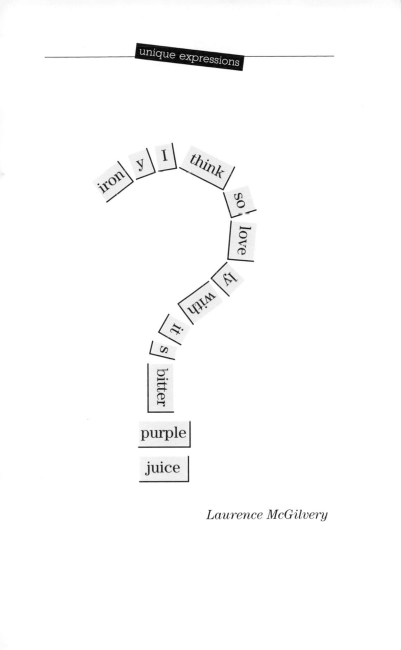

Laurence McGilvery

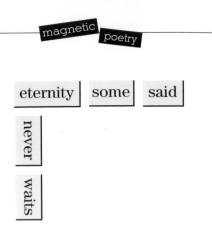

eternity | some | said

never

waits

Andrea Frank

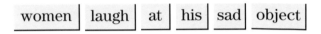

women | laugh | at | his | sad | object

Karena Bauman

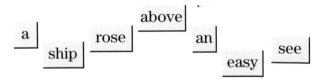

a
ship | rose | above
an | see
easy

Laurence McGilvery

Poetry Primer

Perhaps the first "refrigerator poem" ever written was by William Carlos Williams:

> I have eaten
> the plums
> that were in
> the icebox
>
> and which
> you were probably
> saving
> for breakfast
>
> Forgive me
> they were delicious
> so sweet
> and so cold

At first glance, this poem seems more like a dashed-off apology than verse. But it is deceptively simple. The imagery is vivid, the meaning complex. The poem's rhythm seems as natural as breathing, yet intensifies common speech. We hear every word, see those juicy plums, and know Williams isn't a bit sorry he ate them.

However simple and natural this poem may seem, it's the result of craftsmanship. Like all artists, poets sculpt, refine, and polish their work, using the elements of language

to give special meaning to the ordinary and find awe in the familiar.

Two of these elements are imagery and rhythm. Both come naturally to us—our everyday speech is sprinkled with vivid images and catchy sounds—but can be shaped and trained by listening to the sound of words and their beat when strung together, and by noticing connections between unlikely things.

Writing poetry first requires listening to the sound and meaning of words. Next, since it's rare for a poem to arrive perfectly formed from our minds, it probably needs tinkering and polishing, discarding the extra and extracting the essential, so that the poem we wanted to write (perhaps without even realizing it) emerges.

One way to bring out the poems inside of you, and a good way to become more sensitive to the elements of rhythm and imagery in language, is through writing exercises. These creative "unblockers" are an excellent starting point for new poets and a place writers like to return to now and then.

Once you're off and writing, you may want to explore the other elements of poetic language—rhyme, meter, and form—that have been refined and codified over the centuries.

Rhyme and meter connect poetry with singing and speech; some poetic forms derive from epic storytelling. While it's true that modern poetry veers strongly in the direction of free verse (poetry without rhyme, meter, or form), poets often study the old forms and still write in them in order to learn from their predecessors. In this primer, we'll describe these elements and offer up some examples of poetic forms that work especially well for magnetic poets.

There are six sections here: Creative Exercises; Magnetic Specialties; Poetic Elements; Shapes and Forms; Magnetic Party Poems; and Magnetic Compounds. Each section offers a slightly different approach, or a new tool. Try them out, and use the ones you like.

CREATIVE EXERCISES
Here is a grab bag of ideas to help you get started or send you off in new directions. These writing workouts will sharpen your ear and focus your eye. They'll tone your poetic muscles. After you've tried some of them, explore the further exercises found in Shapes and Forms.

A few rules for exercises:
- Don't worry about rules (there aren't any!)
- Don't try to be brilliant.
- Don't sit around and think.

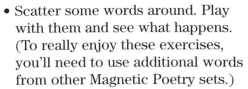

- Scatter some words around. Play with them and see what happens. (To really enjoy these exercises, you'll need to use additional words from other Magnetic Poetry sets.)
- Go for vivid images, silly sounds, strong emotions, musical rhythms, unlikely comparisons, pure nonsense.
- Write about anything.
- Have fun.

1. Like, A Poem!

Collect a bunch of "like" and "as" word magnets and put them in a pile. Now rummage through the remaining words, either selecting randomly or choosing words that strike you, and build similes—phrases that make comparisons between dissimilar things, using "as" and "like" as links.

Go for comparisons that are offbeat, weird, odd, or startling. Play with the sounds of words. Don't try to be logical or even to make sense. The best similes are often those that spring from the unconscious. For example:

> she walks beside me
> like jazz
> coming over the backyard
> fence on a warm
> Sunday morning

David Mark Greaves

If you get rid of the words "like" and "as,"
and make your comparisons directly, the
images become metaphors. For example:

> poetry is
> smoky corduroys
> purple velvet perfume
> sweet rhythm candy
>
> *Juliet Bishop*

> ship these dresses away
> the spring wind is my gown
>
> *Marileta Robinson*

2. Synesthesia

Write a poem describing one or more colors
according to the five senses (sight, smell,
hearing, taste, touch). For instance, what is
the taste of blue? The sound of red? The
smell of purple? The texture of yellow?
Here is an example:

> green talk
> watered
> the moon's mist
>
> *Leigh Ann Smith*

Now write a poem in which you describe
one sense in terms of another. What is the
taste of a woman's cry? What is the smell of
jazz? Here's an example:

> I hear your skin
> whispering please come in

3. Sound Poems

Write a poem using words chosen solely for their sound; don't worry about the meaning. You'll end up with a creation that focuses attention on the emotional impact of sound, even if it doesn't make literal sense.
For example:

> what luscious goddess
> licks the wind
>
> skinless kisses
> will still
> bitter milk

4. Odes

Write a poem celebrating a person or thing—such as a velvet dress, a juicy peach, a soft bed. For example:

> I worship
> joy girls
> in fast shiny cars
> top down red lips flying hair
> they are angels
> soaring in steel

5. List Poems

Write a poem composed of:
- Three things that drive you crazy.
- Three things you love most.
- Three things you really hate.
- The three ugliest things in the world.

- The three loveliest things in the world.
- The three saddest things in the world.

6. Food Poems
- Create a menu of revenge.
- Create a menu to make someone fall in love with you.
- Create a disgusting menu.
- Write a poem in the shape of a banana, a pear, an ear of corn or an egg.
- Write a poem about something inside the refrigerator.

7. Phrase Poems
Start with a phrase and see where it goes:
> I remember . . .
> I dream . . .
> I ignore . . .
> I worship . . .
> I embrace . . .
> I celebrate . . .

8. Lies, Secrets and Fears
- Write a poem made up of lies.
- Write a poem made up of secrets.
- Write a poem made up of fears.

9. Alphabet Poems
An alphabet poem chooses one word for each letter of the alphabet, in order. You can allow some variations, such as a word beginning with "ex-" to stand for the letter "x." Another variation is to have each line of

the poem begin with the alphabet letter,
which makes for a rather long poem!

a broken cloud drooled elegant feathers

absolutely breathless crossing
dull-as ever freeways,
gazing hotly into
just knicknacks,
lightly molding now, or
pushing queens
round stalled traffic
until verily, we explode,
ye zombies!

10. Ghazal Poems

"Ghazal" is an Arabic word that means "the
talk of boys and girls." Ghazal poems,
which were popular in Persia about a thou-
sand years ago, are about flirting and love.
Here's what characterizes a Ghazal: long-
lined couplets (they needn't rhyme) and a
mystical, musing nature:

come here, love, and swim with me
as gorgeous light plays on the sea

11. Impossible Poems

Ask a question that can't be answered and
then try to answer it. Or describe an impos-
sible object. Here are two examples:

What is smaller than nothing?
No or not.

My marble shadow lies buried
in rock beneath the moon

12. Self-Portrait Poems

Write a poem in which you describe your-
self—what you look like, how you behave.
Be specific. Try to capture your essence in a
few lines. Here are some examples:

I chew my hair
and stare at TV
yellow hair, blue eyes
like a doll
but not

13. One-Two-Three Poems

Write a poem in which the first line consists
of one-syllable words, the second line of
two-syllable words, and the third line of
three-syllable words. If you're up for it, try a
four-syllable word line. Here's an example:

how you weep
after waking
abruptly, bewildered:
eternity

MAGNETIC SPECIALTIES

Certain exercises seem as if they were cre-
ated for Magnetic Poetry—and, in fact,
some actually were created by magnetic
poets and sent in to us. They're fun and can
generate great poems.

1. Unstuck Poems

Write a poem using a clump of words, fresh
from the pouch or a kit. For example, this
clump of word magnets:

mother	essential
through	beneath
smooth	moment

became this poem:

> mother is essential
> through and
> beneath
> every smooth moment

M.K. Streznewski

2. Jigsaw Poems

Write a poem using every single piece in the
set. Pile on the adjectives, scatter plurals,
add adverbs to use up your "y's," sprinkle
"ing" wherever you please. Leftovers can be
mixed together: for example, "er" "as" "er"
becomes "eraser." Or "go" and "d" becomes
"god." (One poet transformed "I" "car" "us"

into the tragic mythic figure, "Icarus.")
Don't forget the versatility of common
words, like "for," "of," and "to," and those
humble prefixes and suffixes.

3. Scramble Poems
Write a poem using ten words. Then
rearrange the words, seeing how many
different poems you can make.

Poem:
> I made a garden
> but one winter
> shadows stayed forever

Variations:
> winter made shadows
> but I stayed
>
> but one winter
> I made shadow gardens
>
> one winter garden
> stayed forever
>
> a garden shadows
> but I winter forever
>
> I garden
> but winter shadows
>
> but I stayed
> forever
> a garden

a garden winter made
stayed forever

forever stayed a garden I made

Original poem and variations
by Gail Wronsky

4. Auto-Poetics
Don't think—just do it. Move the words
around for ten minutes. Arrange them how-
ever you like—in short pairs or long phrases.
Stack them on top of each other like blocks.
String them along as far as you can go. This
is "automatic writing" with the vocabulary
provided. When your time is up, see what
you've got—some surprisingly spontaneous
sequences and probably a few gems, too.

POETIC ELEMENTS
The basic elements of poetry are briefly
explained here. Use them as you would any
creative exercise—as scaffolding for the
building of a poem.

1. Rhythm
There's a natural rhythm to both spoken and
written language; so natural, in fact, that we
take it for granted. Modern poetry draws on
the rhythms of spoken language, for the
most part. Traditional forms of poetry more
often imposed an order on these rhythms.

2. Meter

Structuring a poem's rhythm into recurring units creates a meter, or measure. Sometimes poetry naturally falls into a metered rhythm, but more often the meter is intentional. The four most common metrical units (stressed syllables in boldface) are:

Iambic: She **cried**/ and **cried**/ to **no**/ a**vail**
Trochaic: **I** went/ **skip**ping/ **to** the/ **cor**ner
Anapestic: Never **mind**/ after **all**/ it was
     on/ly a **joke**
Dactylic: **Flib**berty/ **gib**berty/ **make** me a/
     hamburger

As you can see and hear, many phrases fall naturally into one or another kind of unit. To hear the meter within words or within entire poems is to recognize the link between poetry and music.

3. Rhyme

We are all familiar with rhyme since we first encountered Mother Goose. One theory holds that rhyme originated in ancient magical incantations and rites. We certainly know that rhyme makes it easier to remember a poem (or any bit of information, for that matter). Many poets use rhyme, but doing it well is tricky. The "Moon/June" school of rhyme is more appropriate to Tin Pan Alley songwriting than to poetry.

Because it can be difficult to do well, beginners may want to avoid using rhyme. But if you want to express yourself in rhyme, aim for unexpected rhymes in unexpected places. Try rhymes that are close rather than exact (thief/shelf; band/friend; hear/wear; harbor/robber).

Rhyme schemes chart the pattern of end-rhymes in the lines of a poem, labeling each line by its ending sound (A,B,C, etc.). Some common rhyme schemes are AABB, and ABAB.

> the flicker from a lingering flame   A
> sparks from a blazing fire   B
> an ocean of immense champagne   A
> boy—you kindle my desire   B

Annie Bright

Internal rhyme links the sounds of words or syllables within a line, or from within separate lines. The effect can be more subtle.

> searching in a flood of dreams
> splashed with the blood of kings

4. Form

A form is the combination of elements—a meter, a rhyme scheme, number of lines to a verse, a pattern of repetition. A sonnet is a form; so is a limerick.

Closed forms are strict in their require-
ments: a certain number of lines to a verse,
a specific meter, a rhyme scheme. Even
blank (unrhymed) verse is a closed form,
with a meter. Other closed forms are sesti-
nas, villanelles, terza rima, and so forth.
Open forms, or free verse, require none of
these elements or systems, but may use any
of them, and others as well.

The most basic form in English, and one
favored by magnetic poets, is the **couplet,**
a two-line poem or two-line unit of a poem.
The couplet has an end rhyme and may or
may not have a metrical pattern: if it does,
both lines have the same pattern.

> a thousand roses will not do
> I ache for the smell of you

> *Susan Johnson*

A three-line poem is called a **tercet:**

> perhaps yesterday
> was always streaming
> after today

A four-liner is a **quatrain:**

> he climbed in you
> tree woman
> why not give him
> two green secrets

Both of these forms may use varying rhymes and meters.

SHAPES AND FORMS
Counted-syllable or counted-word forms are great for magnetic poetry. Each poem contains a specific number of syllables or words in each line, as well as a specific number of lines.

1. Haiku
A classic Japanese form that is usually translated into 17 syllables in three lines. The first line contains five syllables; the second line, seven syllables; the third, five syllables. Traditionally, nature is the topic.

a wounded bird falls	5
from the branch into my hand	7
open, like my heart	5

2. Tanka
A variation of haiku, the tanka is a five-line poem with a line count of 5,7,5,7, and 7 syllables, respectively.

before you go, please	5
send me sea shells and stormy	7
waves in a big box	5
I will climb inside and swim	7
against the current, and win	7

3. Cinquain
This western version of haiku and tanka

was invented by the poet Adelaide Crapsey (1878–1914). This five-line poem's syllable count is 2,4,6,8,2. Since these lines all have an even number of syllables, the effect of a cinquain is often markedly different from haiku or tanka.

window	2
washers look through	4
glass so high and see in	6
side our lives, they watch and whisper	8
not clean	2

4. Lune

This three-line poem counts words, not syllables. Its count is 3,5,3, which makes the poem physically resemble its name, the French word for moon.

mother rose up	3
and screamed, no red meat	5
in my house	3

5. Lantern

This five-line poem has a word count of 1,3,5,3,1. Like the lune, the form it takes on the page resembles the object it is named for.

if	1
you say life	3
is easy, then you must	5
not have known	3
love	1

6. Concrete Poetry

This approach to poetry makes meaningful shapes out of the words of a poem. There are endless ways to use the visual and typographical possibilities of letters and words on a page to enhance the poem's meaning, or even to give it a second meaning:

pole
that
up
go
I

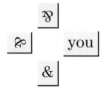

Lawrence McGilvery

MAGNETIC PARTY POEMS

It's a well known fact that Magnetic Poetry inspires great group poems. Here are some ways to use Magnetic Poetry at parties and gatherings, or in daily life.

1. Circulation Poems

At showers and birthdays, reunions and parties, meetings and group therapy sessions, writing a poem together can break the ice, celebrate significant moments, and turn a bunch of strangers into a team. You can use a pizza pan, cookie sheet, door frame, filing cabinet, or the trusty old fridge—any magnetic surface will do. Each person can write a line or everyone can contribute to a group poem. For example:

• At a baby shower in California, a metal tray scattered with magnetic words was passed around. Each guest wrote one line of poetry, and the mother-to-be chose the line she liked best.

• At a group therapy session, clients wrote a poem—each person contributing a word—that described their ordeals and celebrated their endurance.

2. Conversation Poems

Some people use Magnetic Poetry as a sort of bulletin board—not only to leave household messages but to let family and friends know how they're feeling. You can gossip, break important news, apologize, or just let off steam. It's up to each household to decide whether writers are allowed to swipe words from other people's messages in order to make their own. Also up for grabs is whether or not to permit tinkering with someone else's poem—adding new ingredients, revising and changing, so that the poem keeps bubbling like a pot on the stove.

3. Magnetic Corpse

This is a variation of the surrealist parlor game, Exquisite Corpse. Start out by composing one line, plus the first word of the next line, of a magnetic poem. Cover up the completed line, leaving only the single word of the next line visible. Pass it on to the next writer, who repeats the action. Continue the process, with each person adding a line and leaving the first word of the next line exposed. After a dozen or so lines are finished, read the work aloud.

4. How You Say . . .

Pass out a word kit and metal composition board to each person. Have each of them write one event, experience, or thing (such as "eating lunch," "making love," "oversleeping," or "subways") on a slip of paper, fold the paper and put it in a hat. Then each person randomly draws a slip from the hat and writes a few lines from his or her kit about the experience. Trade poems with your neighbors and read them all aloud. Then vote on your favorite and award a point to the winner. Whoever has the most points when the hat is empty is dubbed Poet Laureate of the Living Room. For a variation, try composing in teams.

5. The Poem with a Hundred Arms

The rules of this poetic competition are familiar, but in this variation whole words are used instead of letters. Each player selects ten word tiles and tries to write a whole sentence or phrase with them. You get one point for each tile used; if you use all ten, you get ten bonus points. The next player has to build off the previous sentence. Players can vote on admissibility of sentences—you may want to establish some general rules beforehand.

MAGNETIC COMPOUNDS

Here's a list of some of the compound words you can make with Magnetic Poetry tiles. These words are compound in the sense that they're made of more than one tile bumped together. Now that customizing is possible, it's less crucial that magnetic poets be ingenious about creating compound words. Still, when you feel a poem coming on and need a particular word, it's nice to know you can create it from spare parts.

| he | y | | s | as | s | y | | at | he | ist |

| s | our | | the | or | y | | sweat | er |

| s | is | | d | ing | | live | r | | do | or |

| s | ly | | I | car | us | | for | e | skin |

| r | out | | d | e | a | r | | sno | op |

er | ran | d   t | or | so   must | er

s | in   s | a | me   by | e   her | o

so | used   men | tion   dress | er

no | s | e   or | e | o   me | an   a | men

s | ing   am | use   d | ice   er | r | or

web | sit | e   rock | er   he | a | d

e | we   r | am   s | urge | on

less | on   ed | it | or   he | in | ous

me | and | er | ing   top | I | a | r | y

my | r | I | a | d   so | d   so | r | e | ly

for | age   s | top   no | is | e

s | hot   s | we | a | r   r | over

use|less   s|lick   the|r|a|p|y

s|and   r|est   s|a|d   r|ice

so|r|r|y   car|e   hair|do

r|ing   r|o|am   r|i|d

must|y   her|d   the|at|er

p|ink|y   car|es|s|ed   r|o|me

under|wear   lust|r|ous   d|and|y

a|void   er|r   be|er   er|as|er

s|am   e|r|up|tion   for|a|y

be|ing   d|and|y   d|rip|s

r|a|y   r|a|is|ing   no|tion

butt|er   s|er|en|d|I|p|it|y

MORE WORDS, MORE POETRY

Who knows how many poems you will write in your life? One thing is certain—you'll need more word tiles to express yourself fully. If the many varieties of Magnetic Poetry® aren't available in your local store, if you have suggestions for new words or sets, or if you want to share your poems for future Magnetic Poetry publications, call or write:

Magnetic Poetry
P.O. Box 14862
Minneapolis, MN 55414

1-800-370-7697
magpo@bitstream.net

DAVE KAPELL, inventor of Magnetic Poetry®, was an aspiring songwriter who created it as a way to break through his chronic writer's block.

SALLY STEENLAND is a writer who has been fervently composing Magnetic Poetry poems since she bought her first set.

> The concrete poem on the inside cover, "poetry wakes the breeze," by Sally Steenland, should be read from the bottom up.